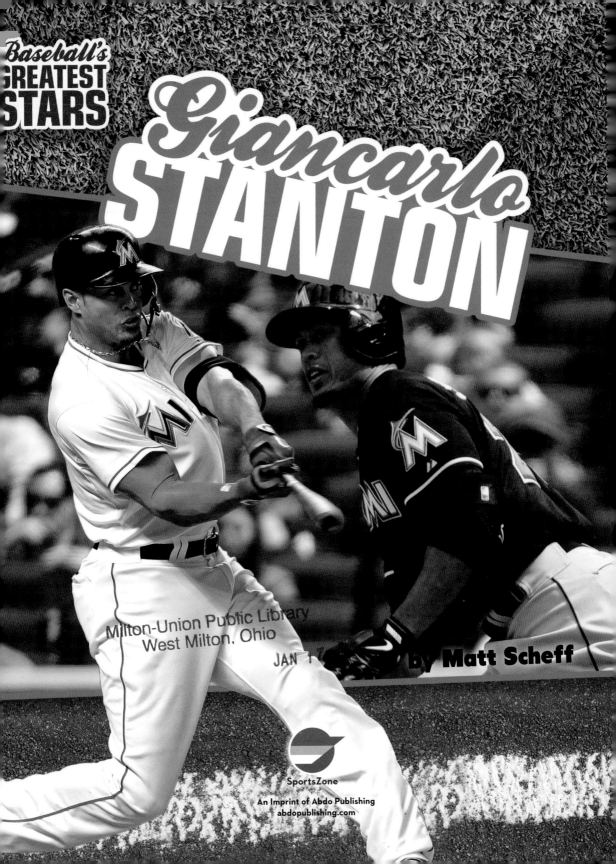

Baseball's GREATEST STARS

Giancarlo STANTON

by Matt Scheff

SportsZone

An Imprint of Abdo Publishing
abdopublishing.com

abdopublishing.com

Published by Abdo Publishing, a division of ABDO, PO Box 398166, Minneapolis, Minnesota 55439. Copyright © 2016 by Abdo Consulting Group, Inc. International copyrights reserved in all countries. No part of this book may be reproduced in any form without written permission from the publisher. SportsZone™ is a trademark and logo of Abdo Publishing.

Printed in the United States of America, North Mankato, Minnesota
082015
012016

Cover Photos: Alan Diaz/AP Images (foreground); Tomasso DeRosa/AP Images (background)
Interior Photos: Alan Diaz/AP Images, 1 (foreground); Tomasso DeRosa/AP Images, 1 (background); Lynne Sladky/AP Images, 4-5, 6-7, 18; Seth Poppel/Yearbook Library, 8-9, 10-11; Matt Slocum/AP Images, 12-13, 16-17, 19; Mike Janes/Four Seam Images/AP Images, 14-15; Tom DiPace/AP Images, 20-21; ZumaPress/Icon Sportswire, 22, 23; Morry Gash/AP Images, 24-25; Hector Gabino/El Nuevo Herald/AP Images, 26-27; Juan Salas/Icon Sportswire, 28; Gene J. Puskar/AP Images, 29

Editor: Patrick Donnelly
Series Designer: Laura Polzin

Library of Congress Control Number: 2015945988

Cataloging-in-Publication Data
Scheff, Matt.
 Giancarlo Stanton / Matt Scheff.
   p. cm. -- (Baseball's greatest stars)
Includes index.
ISBN 978-1-68078-078-9
1. Stanton, Giancarlo--Juvenile literature. 2. Baseball players--United States--Biography--Juvenile literature. I. Title.
796.357092--dc23
[B]   2015945988

CONTENTS

GRAND FINISH

The Miami Marlins and the Seattle Mariners were tied 4-4 in a game early in the 2014 season. It was the bottom of the ninth inning. The bases were loaded. Miami fans stood as star outfielder Giancarlo Stanton stepped to the plate.

Earlier in the game, Stanton had made a throwing error. His mistake had cost the Marlins two runs. This was his chance to make up for it. "Because of what I did earlier in the game . . . it was definitely in my mind as a duty," Stanton said.

Stanton follows through on his big home run against the Mariners.

Stanton made sure his error would not cost the Marlins a win. He took a mighty swing at the pitch. *CRACK!* The crowd went wild as the ball flew off Stanton's bat. It sailed 407 feet and easily cleared the left-field fence. It was a grand slam! Stanton's teammates mobbed him at home plate to celebrate his game-winning blast.

Stanton gets a hero's welcome at home plate after his grand slam beat Seattle in 2014.

EARLY LIFE

Giancarlo Cruz Michael Stanton was born on November 8, 1989, in Panorama City, California. His family is a mix of Puerto Rican, Irish, and African-American heritage. Some people had a hard time pronouncing his name. Many just called him Gene or Carlos. His mom called him Cruz. Around fifth grade, Giancarlo decided that he preferred to be called Mike. The name stuck.

Mike's strong arm made him a great pitcher when he was growing up.

Mike was a standout athlete at Verdugo Hills High School in Tujunga, California. He was a star on the football and basketball teams. He also pitched and played outfield for the baseball team. Before his junior year, Mike transferred to Notre Dame High School in nearby Sherman Oaks, California. He wanted a chance to play for better sports teams. His dad rented an apartment in the area so Mike could attend the school.

FAST FACT
Mike's favorite player as a child was catcher Ivan Rodriguez.

Mike played three sports at Verdugo Hills High School before he transferred.

Many thought Mike's best sport was football. He was a star cornerback and wide receiver for Notre Dame. He had football scholarship offers from several schools. Mike's baseball future seemed less certain. He was very talented and had amazing power at the plate. But his skills were not very polished. Still, Mike liked baseball better, and the Marlins decided to take a chance on him. They selected him in the second round of the 2007 Major League Baseball (MLB) Draft.

Stanton has been part of the Marlins organization since he was drafted in 2007.

MINOR LEAGUER

Stanton signed with the Marlins a few months before he turned 18. He got off to a slow start in the minor leagues. But he found his stroke in 2008. In 125 games with the Greensboro Grasshoppers, Stanton belted 39 home runs. He instantly became one of baseball's hottest outfield prospects.

FAST FACT
After 2008, *Baseball America* ranked Stanton among the top 20 prospects in the minor leagues.

Stanton was just 17 years old when he began his professional career.

Stanton continued to rocket through the Marlins' farm system. In 2009 he played in the MLB All-Star Futures Game. He started 2010 with the Jacksonville Suns. Stanton was unstoppable. He hit 21 home runs in the first two months. One of them went more than 500 feet! The Marlins had seen enough. Stanton was headed to the big leagues.

The Marlins welcomed Stanton to the big leagues on June 8, 2010.

THE BIG LEAGUES

On June 8, 2010, Stanton made his major league debut. He was just 20 years old. In his first game, he got three hits. He also scored two runs.

Ten days later, Stanton stepped to the plate with the bases loaded. Tampa Bay Rays pitcher Matt Garza delivered the pitch. Stanton crushed the ball over the outfield fence. His first big-league home run was a grand slam!

Teammates greet Stanton at home plate after he hit a grand slam for his first major league home run.

Stanton checks in at first base after getting a hit in his first major league at-bat.

FAST FACT

Stanton's teammates call him "Bigfoot" because he is 6 feet 6 inches tall and weighs 240 pounds.

Stanton had become one of the most powerful hitters in the game. Fans loved to watch his monster home runs. In 2011 he slammed five home runs that went at least 455 feet each. In 2012 he hit a grand slam that went 438 feet and knocked out part of a scoreboard! Stanton made his first All-Star Game that season, and he finished the season with 37 home runs.

FAST FACT

Before the 2012 season, Stanton asked to be called Giancarlo again. He thought people would take the time to learn how to pronounce it now that he was a star player.

Stanton pumps his fist after
hitting a big home run in 2012.

Stanton seemed ready for a huge 2013. But he hurt his hamstring early in the season. He missed more than two months. The injury slowed him down. But he still hit a big milestone that year. On June 17, Stanton hit two home runs. That gave him 100 career homers at age 23. Only eight big-league players had reached that mark at a younger age.

Stanton makes a diving catch in right field.

Stanton leaps against the fence in Washington to rob a Nationals player of an extra-base hit.

POWER
AND PAIN

In 2014 Stanton was having his best season yet. On September 11, he led the National League (NL) with 37 home runs. Then he stepped to the plate in the fifth inning of a game against the Milwaukee Brewers. Pitcher Mike Fiers threw a fastball that sailed high and inside. Stanton could not get out of the way. It hit him in the face. Stanton fell to the ground. Team doctors rushed onto the field.

Stanton's season was cut short when a pitch hit him in the face on September 11, 2014.

The pitch had done terrible damage. Stanton had long cuts and broken bones in his face. Several of his teeth also had been knocked out. He did not return to the field that year. Yet despite missing almost a month of the season, he finished second in NL Most Valuable Player voting. The Marlins rewarded him with a new contract. It will pay him $325 million over 13 years. It was the biggest contract in the history of team sports.

FAST FACT

In 2014 Stanton was awarded the NL Hank Aaron Award. The award goes to the best hitter in each league.

Stanton answers questions from the media after he signed his record-setting contract.

Stanton again started out hot in 2015. He lit up the NL with one longball after another. On June 26, he led all of baseball with 27 home runs. But then he broke his wrist in a game against the Los Angeles Dodgers. Another great season had been cut short.

Stanton has struggled with injuries. But no one doubts his ability. Marlins fans look forward to cheering his monster home runs for years to come.

Marlins fans hope to see many home-run trots from Stanton in the near future.

Stanton returned to action in 2015 wearing a mask designed in the shape of a G to protect his jaw.

TIMELINE

1989
Giancarlo Cruz Michael Stanton is born on November 8 in Panorama City, California.

2005
Stanton transfers to Notre Dame High School in Sherman Oaks, California.

2007
Stanton signs with the Marlins after they select him in the second round of the draft.

2008
Stanton belts 39 home runs in his first full minor league season.

2010
Stanton gets three hits in his Major League debut on June 8.

2013
Stanton becomes the ninth-youngest player in MLB history to reach 100 career home runs.

2014
Stanton hits an NL-best 37 home runs. His season ends early after he is hit in the face by a pitch.

2015
Stanton leads all of baseball with 27 home runs before suffering a broken wrist in late June.

GLOSSARY

CONTRACT
An agreement to play for a certain team.

DEBUT
First appearance.

DRAFT
The process by which leagues determine which teams will sign new players coming into the league.

FARM SYSTEM
In baseball, all the minor league teams that feed players to one major league team.

GOLD GLOVE
An award that recognizes the top fielder in the league at each position.

HAMSTRING
Any of five tendons at the back of a person's knee.

HERITAGE
A person's ethnic or cultural background.

PROSPECT
An athlete likely to succeed at the next level.

SCHOLARSHIP
Money given to a student to pay for education expenses.

TRANSFER
To switch schools.

INDEX

ABOUT THE AUTHOR

Matt Scheff is an artist and author living in Alaska. He enjoys mountain climbing, deep-sea fishing, and curling up with his two Siberian huskies to watch baseball.